Phillips
COLLECTORS GUIDES

TOY SOLDIERS

Text ©   James Opie
Illustration ©   Phillips Fine Art
                 Auctioneers
Edited by   Emma Sinclair-Webb
Designed by   Strange Design Associates

Boxtree Ltd.
36 Tavistock Street
London WC2 7PB

Conceived by Dunestyle Publishing Ltd

ISBN 1 85283 249 5

Typesetting by O'Reilly Clark, London
Colour separation by Chroma Graphics
(Overseas) Pte Ltd
Printed In Italy by New Interlitho spa.

COLLECTORS GUIDES

TOY SOLDIERS

JAMES OPIE

BOXTREE

Phillips

WEST TWO

Phillips, founded in 1796, has a reputation for specialisation. Its specialists handle fine art, antiques and collectors' items under more than 60 subject headings — a huge spectrum of art and artefacts that ranges from Old Masters and the finest antique furniture to cigarette cards and comparatively modern pop memorabilia. The auction group's Collectors' Centre, situated at Phillips West Two in Salem Road, Bayswater, London, is constantly recognising, defining and catering for new trends in collecting. It answers hundreds of queries a day from collectors, museums, dealers and the public at large. The shelves of its cataloguing halls are packed with a treasure-trove of objects, awaiting their turn to appear at auction. To varying extents, the scene there and in the main Mayfair salerooms (Phillips, 7 Blenheim Street, London W1Y 0AS; telephone 01-629 6602) is repeated at a score of Phillips branches elsewhere in Britain.

Phillips continues today the only series of regular specialist toy soldier auctions in the world, in London and New York. About 50,000 figures a year are offered in these auctions, a series which has lasted for over twenty years and forms one of the principal focuses of the collection scene.

Phillips West 2
10 Salem Road
London W2 4BU
Telephone: 01-221 5303

Contents

Introduction

The Fascination of Toy Soldiers

Enter the world of the Toy Soldier! Colourful royal guards, heroic soldiers in action, the navy, the air force, knights in armour, cowboys and indians or presidential parades: they are all there to be collected, perused, analyzed and arranged. Many collectors are at first re-entering a world that gave them pleasure as children, but at the adult level the subject is equally popular, its fascination more fully appreciated.

Toy soldiers represent the pivotal place that the soldier has in society. Weapons for hunting were probably the first tools ever used by mankind, and set the race on the road to civilization. The subsequent use of armaments to settle dominance quarrels between individuals and tribes or nations is arguably the most important strand of our entire history. Certainly, the earliest historians, from Homer onwards, emphasized the enormous importance of war and its

outcome.

Miniature reproductions of the military have had a myriad of uses, from the funerary armies of ancient Egypt and China to medieval jousting models, the instructional squadrons of princes and the war-gaming tables of modern staff colleges. As soon as mass production and distribution methods were available, toy soldiers in various forms became available for children to play with. More attractive and cheaper than home made or locally produced toys, they were eagerly bought by children and parents alike.

Toy soldiers for children have since then proliferated into many forms, as indeed have more intricate and supposedly accurate models for adults. The toys, however, have a simplistic charm that often makes them better looking than the more serious military miniatures.

In the following pages, after reviewing the types of toy soldier

by main methods of manufacture, today's collecting market is examined. Current prices to be expected, trends, rarities and items of outstanding interest form a large part of the knowledge with which collectors should be equipped. Thus armed, each can follow his own inclinations. The enormous variety available allows for a wide choice of collecting possibilities, providing the chance to explore new ground or to collect from many diverse areas. The book includes two case studies of collections; these are intended to give an idea of the level of complexity that can be achieved in a small collection and in the collecting of the world's most popular toy soldiers: those produced by Britains Ltd.

This book is designed as a guide to the scope, expense and activity associated with collecting toy soldiers. There are, indeed, as yet few reference books on the subject, and these as well as other general reading are included in the bibliography.

The heroic image of the soldier as the champion of society is still as evident in today's toys as it has ever been: nowadays manifested in models of Star Wars, Masters of the Universe and hundreds of similar fictional scenarios. The discontinued plastic toy soldiers of twenty years ago are now becoming collectable – it looks as though the possibilities are unlimited.

Left Britains armoured car. Britains motor vehicles tended to be rather smaller than the 54 mm size, and were by no means as elaborate as their German equivalent.

Below The vehicles made in tinplate to accompany the Hausser and Lineol 70 mm size German Army figures are among the most beautiful toys ever made. The Mercedes SS Staff car sold for £400/$792 in 1984.

Below, middle Heyde Royal Engineers semaphore signallers in 45 mm size. Heyde, as with most German toy soldier makers, made far more animated figures than most of Britains, which tended to confine themselves to drill positions. Eight similar figures sold for £120/$216 in 1984.

Bottom The first box of Britains toy soldiers. The models are slightly smaller than the later 54 mm size of Britains standard figures. This box was sold at Phillips for £550/$990 in 1984.

Chapter One

Types of Soldiers

Commercial toy soldiers have been generally available from the mid-eighteenth century, and in such a vast variety of styles that no collection will ever be exhaustive.

Flat Figures and Solid Figures

Toy soldiers vary in their representational effect between two dimensions and three. The paper cut-out was the first form of two dimensional figure; at the other end of the scale is the fully three dimensional solid figure, the most developed of military miniatures and still produced for the adult market. A figure in metal or plastic with relief of less than 2 mm is normally considered a 'flat', any toy that can be viewed from all round to equal effect is deemed a 'solid', and anything in between the two is termed a 'semi-flat' or 'semi-solid'.

Sizes

The conventional method of denoting the size of a toy soldier is to measure, in millimetres, the height of the standing figure from the top of his head without hat to the sole of his feet, not including the thickness of any base on which he might be standing.

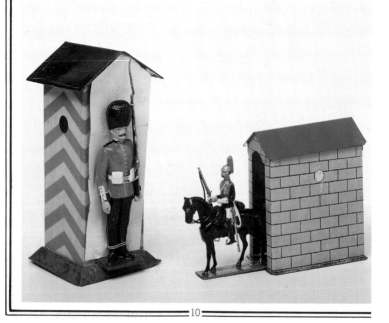

Toys and Models Compared

Below left German-made sentries with tinplate sentry boxes, probably by Heyde. The Foot Guard is 120 mm size and sold for £330/$594 in September 1987. The Horse Guard is 60 mm size and sold for £340/$612 in the same sale. Both are superb examples of the best work of the German toymakers.

Below A supreme example of the modelmakers art; Napoleonic First Empire, 54 mm size, *Garde Impériale Tartares Lithuaniens Trompette* 1812 by Roger Berdou. This model sold for £180/$324 in September 1987 and represents the top end of the range of prices for models. To put it in perspective: in the same sale, mounted Stadden figures in the same size, painted to the highest standard, were being sold for an average of £20/$36 each, about one third of their retail price.

Below A box of semi-flat soldiers in 40 mm size. Depicting Indian camel lancers, these are a rare example of collectable semi-flat figures. All too often, semi-flats are home-cast from moulds sold for the purpose, and virtually worthless. This boxed set, on the other hand, with its charming label showing two boys playing, and dating from the turn of the nineteenth century, sold for £160/$288 in 1984.

Below right Heyde 45 mm size, pieces from an Indian Durbar display, with elephants, camels, carts, palm trees and Indian Army Infantry. Large set pieces of this nature show Heyde at their best. This collection sold for £1,350/$2,430 in 1984.

The Major Manufacturing Methods – presented chronologically.

Flat Tin Soldiers

Flat figures in a tin and lead alloy were the first to be mass-produced. Made from engraved slate moulds, they were produced in Nuremburg, Germany, by an industry that originated in the sixteenth century. The early pioneer who arranged distribution and export of large numbers of the flat figures was Johann Gottfried Hilpert (1732-1801). The normal size of those figures was 50 mm to 60 mm tall. This has remained the favourite size for toy soldiers ever since, although for those enthusiasts interested in more individual detail, larger models have also been made. Alternatively, it is possible to acquire smaller figures produced for the collector of whole armies!

Flat figures have remained in production to this day, despite the fact that over the period 1880 to 1920 they were largely superseded as toys by the solid figures. Since then the art and artistry of flat figures has been kept alive by adult collectors, and there is sufficient demand to sustain the production of new models and reissues of old ones. In Europe many major collections are made up of, or include, substantial numbers of flat figures. There is less interest in these through the rest of the world and flat figures come up at auction in London and New York relatively infrequently.

Major manufacturers of flat figures include: *Germany* – Hilpert, Heinrichsen, Allgeyer, Haffner, Ochel; *France* – Mignot.

Solid Lead Soldiers

The earliest commercial maker of the solid lead figure before 1789 is generally acknowledged to be Lucotte of Paris, although detailed evidence of this has not been substantiated but is based on the tradition of the successor firm of Mignot. At the time of writing Mignot still maintains a precarious existence in Paris.

The early figures were fully solid, 52 mm in size, cast in a lead, tin and antimony alloy, and by the mid-nineteenth century were well known throughout Europe. Their quality today remains extremely high and production is expensive as it involves soldering many joints to make up all the parts and accoutrements of the figure.

The traditional rivalry between France and Germany in toy making encouraged a number of German manufacturers to make solid figures of a quality that, in the best examples, matched the

Below Hausser and Lineol 70 mm size toy soldiers included many models of Nazi party organization figures, and prominent personalities. Although these have unpleasant associations, they are a faithful representation of this period of German history. This is a group of Lineol figures; left to right, German Army Regimental Standard (£50/$90), Hitler in party uniform (£32/$57), Goering in party uniform (£42/$75), Von Mackensen in Hussar full dress (£42/$75), Mussolini mounted (£110/$198) and German army Third Reich standard (£75/$135). They were all sold at Phillips in June 1988.

Bottom Mignot 54 mm size, a scenic display box of an air base with early monoplanes, French air crew and spectators. The scenery is cast semi-flat, and details like spare propellors and petrol cans are included. This set sold at Phillips for £750/$1,350, in October 1988.

French production. German manufacturers produced figures of different size and varying quality. Semi-flat figures were also produced, one variation being solid cavalry figures mounted on semi-flat horses. The major German firm was Heyde of Dresden. Both French and German solid figures have been widely exported, and these figures have a considerable following among collectors at the top end of the market.

Major manufacturing names are: *France* – Lucotte, CBG Mignot; *Germany* – Heyde, Heinrich, Haffner.

Hollowcast Lead Soldiers

In 1893 William Britain first started manufacturing and distributing, in Britain, toy soldiers made by a new casting process. This enabled the interior of the figure to be left hollow by pouring the still-molten metal out of the mould, leaving behind a shell that formed the model. The new process cut the raw material cost

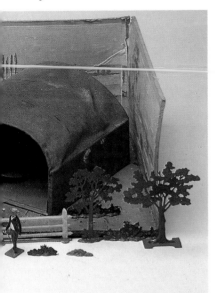

by half and boosted sales of figures of all qualities to previously unrealized levels. Gamages of Holborn, for instance, announced a stock of half a million figures!

Manufacturers using the hollowcast method soon spread in Britain and the process was later adopted in the United States and France. From 1900 to 1955 this method of production was the most commonly-used throughout the world. Most of the larger British companies exported widely, especially to the English-speaking world.

In the USA, a sub-type of hollowcast toy soldier was created by the two firms of Barclay and Manoil, with a number of lesser makers participating. They are chunky-looking hollowcast figures manufactured from the 1930s to the 1950s and mainly depicting US servicemen. In 70 mm size, they were available in 'five and dime' stores (stores selling items at five or ten cents apiece) and are thus known as 'Dime Store' figures. There are many keen collectors of these models in the United States, but they rarely appear elsewhere.

Major manufacturing names are: *Britain* – Britains, Hill, Reka, BMC, Fry, Crescent, Timpo; *France* – *Mignot*; *USA* – Barclay, Manoil.

Composition Soldiers

In about 1900, experiments in Germany resulted in a method of manufacturing toy soldiers from a material called composition, a mixture of sawdust, casein, kaolin and glue, moulded round a wire frame and baked. The predominent size of these figures, made in the 1900-1955 period, was 70 mm, but larger (100 mm) and smaller versions (60 mm to 40 mm) were also made, and sizes were not consistent. The principle manufacturer was Hausser, whose composition material was known

as Elastolin and became a generic name for the figures.

Major manufacturing names are: *Germany* – Hausser, Lineol, Leyla; *Belgium* – Durso.

Aluminium Soldiers

In the late 1930s, a process that used sand moulds for producing solid aluminium figures was invented in France. The idea was taken up by one major manufacturer in Britain in about 1948, but the process did not have a great impact on the toy market as by this time plastic was proving a more versatile material.

Major manufacturing names are: *France* – Quiralu; *Britain* – Wend-Al.

Plastic Soldiers

Plastic moulded soldiers first started to be made shortly after the Second World War, and during the period 1953 to 1963 effectively ousted all other forms of toy soldiers from the commercial toy market. Injection moulding was capital-intensive, but produced very large quantities of extremely cheap and ostensibly unbreakable figures. The hand-painting of toy soldiers was also time-consuming and, therefore, expensive, with the result that there was a trend to marketing the soldiers unpainted, or experimenting with fit-together self-coloured parts.

At the same time, plastic mouldings could be used to produce much better animated figures with extremely thin parts, that might be flexible but would not break off as easily as those of a metal figure. So good have these models now become, that they are closer to scale models than toys. Although they are still played with by children, they are also incorporated into detailed models or used for war-games by older children and adults.

Major manufacturing names are: *Britain* – Herald, Timpo, Crescent, Cherilea, Airfix, Lone Star, Britains; *USA* – Marx; *France* – Starlux; *Spain* – Reamsa; *Italy* – Nardi, Atlantic, Esci; *Germany* – Hausser, Merten.

Modern Solid Soldiers

During the twentieth century there has been considerable adult interest in toy soldiers, initially as a basis for producing spectacular mass models and dioramas of military actions and, later, as collectables in their own right. The first interest has produced, over the last forty years, a plethora of accurate models, the majority of which are not regarded as collectables – apart from their value as *objets d'art* – by anyone else but their initial purchaser. They, therefore, have a second-hand value only. Collecting toy soldiers has resulted in a lively market, now of some twenty years standing, complete with its own periodicals, literature, dealers and auctions. Furthermore, there are a sufficient number of collectors for modern manufacturers to produce toy-style figures aimed at the collecting market rather than at children. These collectors' figures, or 'new toy soldiers' as they are called, are normally made of solid tin and lead alloy in the tradition of Mignot, but with new and distinctive design characteristics that range from the crude to the sophisticated. The toy-like appearance is retained in the simplicity of the design, glossy painting and such conventions as movable arms.

Early attempts at this sort of figure were made in the early 1950s by Authenticast and Carman among others. They intended to introduce greater variety to the existing range of toy soldiers, but because of the continuing availability of commercial toy soldiers in large quantities, they were not greatly successful. The 'new toy soldier' only became a success some twenty years after the general demise of the commercial metal toy soldier, but

Left Boxes from sets of different quality and sizes of Britains toy soldiers. All these boxes contained small 43 mm size figures. The top box is poor quality and anonymous – Britains did not include their trademark in the label design. The second box is from the 'W' range of small size second grade figures. The box at the bottom is set 15b, best quality painted small size figures. Four cavalry sold for half the price of the five cavalry in standard size box.

since 1972 scores of small enterprises have been started in Britain and the USA, and Britains Ltd have themselves developed a new range of die-cast metal figures aimed at the collector, souvenir and toy markets.

Major manufacturing names are: *Eire* – Authenticast; *Spain* – Alymer; *Britain* – Carman, Mark Time, Blenheim, Nostalgia, Bulldog, Ducal, Tradition, Trophy, Dorset, Bastion, Marlborough; *New Zealand* – Imperial; *USA* – Imrie, Hocker, Scruby.

Toy soldiers have also been made from tin plate, paper, cardboard, *papier mâché*, soap, plaster, china, rubber, wood and many other materials.

Quality and Grades

Most manufacturers catered for different markets, offering everything from enormous sets of boxed best quality soldiers for the very rich to inexpensive, unpainted soldiers for people to decorate themselves. CBG Mignot specialized in scenic layout boxes, with backgrounds printed inside the box and the soldiers and scenery fixed in realistic positions. The box could be stood up like a picture.

Britains' best quality toy soldiers are painted in up to twelve different colours, while less well-produced varieties might be decorated with six, five or only four colours. Gilt figures were simply painted gold; these were the cheapest of all. Britains' less expensive lines were based on simpler castings, the figures were smaller and there were fewer figures in a box. Many competitors did the same. German manufacturers tended to produce their best figures to a higher standard than Britains; their models were larger and were extremely well painted, in the tradition of the German toy-makers. Theirs are probably the most intrinsically attractive toy soldiers ever produced, and are extremely rare and expensive today. For instance, a guardsman and sentry box in its original box cost £260/$468 in 1987. The Germans also produced the cheapest toy soldiers: the 27 mm size, unpainted flat figures.

Toy Soldiers Available at Auction at Phillips, London

Approx. proportions	By Quantity %	By Value %
Britains Hollowcast	30	60
Other British Hollowcast	35	10
Mignot	3	6
Compostion	5	9
German Solids	2	4
Flats	5	2
Plastic	10	3
New Toy Soldiers	10	6
	100	100

Below Both Lineol and Hausser normally marked figures underneath the bases, the Hausser figures including the word 'Elastolin', their trademark for the material from which they were made. In addition, Lineol normally had square bases, and Elastolin round bases, so that the three figures on the right can easily be seen to be Elastolin. The two firms were great rivals with Lineol seeming to produce marginally the better quality – compare the two portraits of Hitler. Many figures were produced by each in almost identical poses. These sold at Phillips in May 1988 for a total of £670/$1,200.

Chapter Two

Advice for Collectors

When presented with a figure, the collector of toy soldiers should attempt to identify the manufacturer, detect any repairs and embellishments and spot conversions.

The first thing to do is look at the base of the figure, as this is where Britains and many other manufacturers identify their figures. If there is no lettering underneath, there may be some elsewhere, so it is worth a careful look. It is important to acquire an eye for the style of a figure through details of sculpture and paintwork; this will enable an attribution to be made with some confidence, even when there are no marks.

During the period 1897 to 1908, many early British manufacturers of toy soldiers were making blatant copies or extremely similar figures to those produced by Britains Ltd. This was caused by ex-Britains employees starting up on their own account and many were successfully prosecuted. This was not to be the sole instance of copying or piracy occurring in the toy soldier trade – there was another rash of it when early plastics were copied in Hong Kong. The Britains copy figures are often made out of brighter, more brittle metal than Britains' own metal; they have rougher edges and thinner, more powdery paint. Often, small details of moulding are enough to identify a copy from an original. For instance, Britains' horses do not have moulded saddle girths where one prominent copy does. Copies and piracies are an interesting subject to collect in their own right.

Style and colour of paint are even more important features to notice when looking for imperfections in figures. Collectors are willing to pay high prices for rare figures in original paint; any figure that has been re-painted will be worth considerably less. Original purchasers often embellished the figure's uniform with additional detail, such as insignia on the sleeve, a shoulder strap, an extra belt, piping and webbing, silvering on metal weapons or a rifle strap. By studying displays of soldiers where the originals are known – for example, at an auction viewing – the habitual standard of paintwork can be recognized, and any embellishments will become apparent.

Repairs almost inevitably involve slight sculptural alterations to the figures: a difference to the angle of a leg, for example, or a change in the thickness of a neck. After a repair a slight touching up of the paintwork is usually needed. Modern paints are completely

Below This interesting group of 45 mm size figures, probably by Heyde, certainly solid cast and made in Germany, had an interesting but probably incorrect label with them. They sold for £850/$1,530 in 1984.

different from those in use before about 1955; they are more opaque, and of a different sheen and touch. Differences are very often quite easily evident, but, if they are not, many new paints will show up under a fluoroscope.

Conversions involve the changing of a figure to a different one by means of changing heads, arms or other parts. It is possible to convert a common Britains figure to a very rare one, simply by repainting. It is, therefore, most important to be familiar with Britains' habitual shades of green for bases and metallic brown for rifles – the two most difficult paint shades to reproduce – in order to spot standard figures masquerading as rarer examples.

Repainting should never be carried out in an attempt to try to improve an original figure: it invariably reduces the value to collectors. Repairing and repainting in order to provide a mass display at small cost, however, is perfectly legitimate.

The recasting of original toys, sometimes making modifications to heads and arms, is another

Below British Infantry at Waterloo, the only British troops of the Napoleonic era made by Mignot. These twelve figures sold for £90/$162 in 1988.

Right Mignot 54 mm size Highlander marching. Foreign manufacturers tended to produce a limited range of British troops, but the famous Highlanders were nearly always featured.

common activity among the more skilled collector. Home-casting kits are available, although their products are not always very satisfactory. But, nicely finished and painted recasts can be just as much works of art as the original toys, and they enable somewhat uninspiring ranks of toys to be equipped with officers, musicians or anything else the collector requires. Recasting is almost invariably done as solids, so picking up a figure that is surprisingly heavy can reveal a recast that, in all other ways, looks original.

All restored, repaired or recast figures have a value based on their aesthetic qualities, and equivalent to the amount of time and patience that a buyer would have to expend in order to achieve a similar result. A poorly converted item has no value other than as a basis for further conversion. The original base material for these figures appears at auction in lots of broken pieces. A hundred of these examples can be purchased for as little as £50/$90. The finished work of an expert such as Freddie

Green, on the other hand, will sell for as much as £20/$36 per figure.

Some collectors have turned professional designers, producing new toy soldiers in the traditional poses. These are available by post or through collector's shops for about £5/$9 each for foot figures (see page 17, *Modern Solid Soldiers*).

The collecting of all the different versions and variations in which an item was produced by the manufacturers exerts a fascination for many people. The idea behind this is to start with a particular set of figures, many of which were produced over a period of seventy or more years, and then acquire examples of the same set with the various changes in manufacture, the differences in mould, paint finish and even box labels.

The products of Britains Ltd are those most commonly collected in this way (see Chapter Seven, where examples are given of the complexities involved).

Collecting Imperatives –
The Do's and Don'ts

Do:

1. Do buy what you like the look of; it will always give you enjoyment, and what you enjoy will be most likely to please others.

2. Do travel to collect examples. Toy soldiers can be more expensive in the country of origin, but they will also be much more plentiful. Attending auctions in person enables the lots to be inspected and the purchases to be taken home safely.

3. Do give figures room to breath on display. A 54 mm size infantryman will have a base approximately 1 cm^2 to 2 cm^2, and ten figures will be able to be lined up within 20 cm (8 in). At least a 10 cm (4 in) gap should be left between this and the next subject.

4. Do keep original boxes, which will enhance the value by up to 100 per cent. (See chapter on prices, page 26).

5. Do make sure any cupboards or cabinets have sufficient ventilation. Damp conditions in sealed enclosures cause damage to lead figures.

6. Do try to purchase soldiers in the best condition that you can afford.

7. Do learn, as much as possible, which are rarities. Your knowledge will be pitted against the auctioneers, dealers and other collectors.

Don'ts:

1. Don't send toy soldiers through the post unless unavoidable. When packing, use plenty of tissue paper, and pack tightly round with bubble-pack or newspaper so that the models cannot move about in transit.

2. Don't believe that plastic figures are unbreakable. Some of the plastic used was mixed with chalk to aid paint adhesion, and is extremely brittle. Careful handling is also necessary to prevent the paint flaking off. Altogether, plastics that are not chewed, nicked, bent, warped, split, scuffed or melted – in other words, those in pristine condition – are considerably rarer than the equivalent metal models.

3. Don't buy semi-solid home-cast figures; they are usually worthless.

4. Don't store lead alloy figures in oak furniture. Oak secretes tannic acid which attacks the lead.

5. Don't feel that condition is all important – if something fits in a collection, buy it, even if it is imperfect. The perfect example may or may not be available later, and if it is, the first can be sold again.

Middle and bottom This magnificent set 44 by Britains is made to a horse design nicknamed the Rocking Horse, because of its unrealistic pose with all four legs outstretched. The German-made Heinrich set of Horse Guards below it appear at first sight to be of the same design. The most obvious difference to be seen in the photogrphs is the shape of the plume. When these figures are not in their boxes, it is difficult to determine the maker, since neither are marked with any lettering. Perhaps the same designer made master models for them both – the similarity can hardly be a coincidence. All we know is that the Heinrich hollowcast models are much rarer than the Britains, so Britains won the commercial struggle easily on its home ground.

Left Britains often used one basic figure for more than one set. The figure on the left is a German Infantryman in steel helmet, introduced in 1931, and in 1939 the figure was used, among others, for Polish and Netherlands Infantry (right). The Pole has the same bowl-shaped helmet as the Dutchman, but this is the rarer Netherland figure, as the Polish uniform is a slate blue colour rather than the olive green of the Dutch. A set of Germans is worth £80/$144, a set of Poles £150/$270 and a set of Netherlands Infantry £500/$900, so it is obviously worth examining any purported Netherlanders very carefully in case they are repainted Poles or converted Germans. Should the same Polish figure be found in a brown uniform, it is the even rarer Argentine Infantry *con casco*, worth £800/$1,440 a set.

Chapter Three

Prices

Prices

Toy soldier sets are nearly all currently worth anything between £20/$36 and £10,000/$18,000 each; individual figures range in value from 50 pence/90 cents to upwards of £50/$90 for a rare figure. The average lot at auction is now £100/$180 and it is still possible to pick up lots of quite good hollowcast figures to repair and repaint for less than £1/$1.80 per figure.

The most expensive auction for toy soldiers, at the time of writing, was that held on 9 and 10 September 1987; it included the collection of John G. Garratt, the toy and model soldier encyclopedist.

The auctioneering of toy soldiers as a speciality has just celebrated its 20th anniversary, and comparison of prices for some items is instructive. Here is an idea of the prices, over a period of time, for a boxed common set, a rarer standard set and a highly sought-after set:

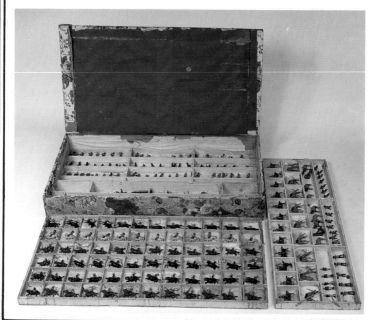

Below left The most expensive box of toy soldiers, set 131, was the largest box ever made by Britains Ltd. and contained 275 figures. In January 1987, this set, which has been quite well played with, and has 114 pieces damaged and 30 missing, sold at Phillips for £10,000/$18,000. This gives an average price of £37/$66.60 per figure, not all that high compared with Lord Strathcona's Horse (see page 29) which cost £320/$576 per figure, over eight times as much.

Below This is set 75, Scots Guards at the slope. The set has oval bases, the second version of this figure made from 1905 to 1909, and is thus quite rare, but, as can just be seen, the man on the extreme left has a square base, and so this set is not properly matched. Had the set been perfect, it could well reach £300/$540 at auction, in view of its age, but, since it has imperfections and it is a common set, the expected price in 1989 would be £100/$180.

	New in	1969 price	1979 price	1989 price
Britains Cossacks, set 136	1959 – 50p/90 cents	£6/$11	£40/$72	£90/$162
Britains Duke of Cornwall's Light Infantry, set 2088	1959 – 50p/90 cents	£8/$14	£75/$135	£300/$540
Britains Royal Marines, Tropical Dress, set 1619	1937 – 9p/16 cents	£12/$22	£100/$180	£1,800/$3,240

All prices quoted from auctioneers' records are *without* the buyer's premium or value added tax, which together usually add 11½ per cent to the overall cost.

The prices quoted are for near perfect examples, and in the original boxes where they are boxed sets. As with most collectables, the condition of paint and the absence of damage is extremely important to value. Mint boxed sets, to take an example, of Greek Cavalry by Britains, sell for up to £1,000/$1,800, while a damaged set in fair condition would only fetch £200/$360. It is part of the expertise of the auctioneer to judge how attractive a set will be, in terms of the price it will achieve, whether in mint or poor paint condition and whether with minor or major damage. Estimates for lots on sale will reflect condition – the terminology used to describe the condition is explained in the sale catalogue

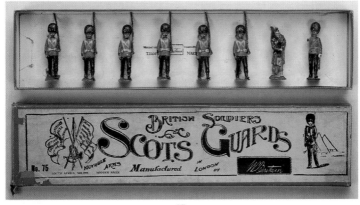

Below It is extremely rare to find Hausser or Lineol composition figures in their boxes. This orange lid with Lineol label, with its trademark of three goose-stepping geese, is worth at least £50/$90 without any of the contents of the box.

Bottom Britains set 1904, one of the very few single row sets worth over £1,000/$1,800. This one sold for £1,600/$2,880 in 1988.

Below Britains set 1629, Lord Strathcona's Horse, current holder of the world auction record for a standard single row box of five cavalry, fetching £1,800/$3,240

introduction. The above estimates are a good indication of the sort of price that has been achieved before, but, in competitive bidding situations, rare items can often go far above them.

Packaging

Not all collectors like to collect the boxes in which the soldiers were originally sold, but those who do are prepared to pay a much higher price. The box completes the set as it was manufactured, and mint toy soldiers are defined as those that have never been taken out of their box.

Britains' sets normally come as eight infantry or five cavalry in a single row box, and boxed sets are common. Nevertheless, it is normal to find that sets in original boxes are between 50 per cent to 100 per cent more expensive than those without. Large display boxes are rarer, but are not necessarily more expensive *pro rata* as few collectors have room for them. Boxes of cheaper quality soldiers are also rarer, as the boxes were more often thrown away and a higher proportion of cheap toy soldiers were sold loose in the shops rather than boxed. Because cheap toy soldiers are less collected than Britains, boxed sets of these are less expensive than Britains' boxed sets.

However, the premium for them over the unboxed figures is higher than it is for Britains' boxed sets over Britains' unboxed figures. Thus for Crescent figures, six foot guards separately might cost £7/$13, while the same figures in their original box might cost £25/$45.

Even rarer than the original boxes is display material created for shops, and not available to the general public. Britains catalogues give details of some examples.

Auction Records: Britains Ltd

The highest price paid for a single set of toy soldiers was £10,000/$18,000 for a set 131, auctioned in January 1987, the biggest set ever produced by Britains. Had this set, which contains 273 pieces, been in better condition, it might well have sold for twice the amount.

Below Britains British Camel Corps. From 1981 to 1987 this figure held the world record for the sale at auction of a single toy soldier, at £250/$450. In fact, the offering of single figures at auction is quite rare, as such items are usually parts of sets. The British Camel Corps was only available in set 131, which contained nine. As models, they are exactly the same as the Egyptian or Bikanir Camel Corps, but with a different head. This makes them rather easy to fake.

The highest price paid for an artillery team was £7,200/$12,960 for set 1339, the Royal Horse Artillery in steel helmets, at an auction in January 1985. This set was in virtually perfect condition.

The highest price paid for a single five-piece set of cavalry dating from the pre-1916 era was £1,500/$2,700 for a box of Boer Cavalry, set 6, at an auction in March 1988.

The highest price paid for a single-row box of soldiers was £3,800/$6,840 for a set of 'Germanic' Royal Fusiliers, lot 132 in the Phillips sale of May 1984.

The highest price paid for a single five-piece set of cavalry was £1,800/$3,240 for set 1629, Canadian Lord Strathcona's Horse, in May 1988.

The highest price paid for a mounted band was £2,600/$4,680 for a red-jacketed Life Guards

Below Britains Model Fort. Once there is a body of collectors intent on acquiring all the known products of a particular company, then the rarer items become sought after and expensive, particularly if they are interesting and attractive. For a few years in the 1930s Britains offered for sale this colour printed cardboard fort, which was sold in a paper envelope. Although many other similar forts were on sale, because this was made by Britains it has a much enhanced value. Britains also included it, as here, in double row sets of soldiers. Note that the drawing of the fort on the envelope is not nearly as representative of the actual toy as the drawing on the box label. This set 1394 was sold at Phillips in October 1988 for £6,000/$10,800. With sets as rare as this, the splits along the sides of the box lid will not affect the price.

Below and right Britains aircraft are much sought after – illustrated here, set 1521, Biplane (£3,800/ $6,840 in 1984) and set 1431 Autogiro (£2,100/ $3,780 in 1988). The only comparable prices for other makers' aircraft are the tinplate German-made Tippco aircraft.

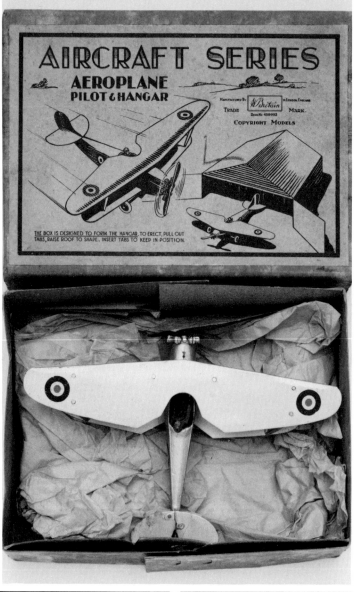

Bottom A Britains monoplane in less good condition, with the hangar box made up. This plane has its propeller blades missing and sold for just £120/$216 in 1981. Even allowing for rising prices, this shows the advantages of perfect condition.

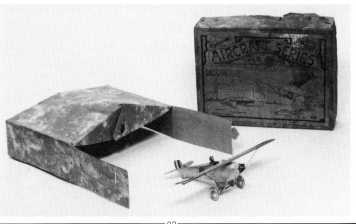

These pages In 1907 Britains issued two sets with patent clips to hold the soldiers. These had been invented by Charles William Beisser, who then used Britains soldiers in many sets issued by his American Soldier Company in New York. Sold in 1988, set 148, Royal Lancaster Regiment, fetched

£3,200/$5,760 and set 149, American soldiers, £3,800/$6,840. To show that prices do not always go up, set 148 was sold without its box for £3,200/$5,760 in 1984. The 'American Hero' set is typical of the Beisser chip sets issued in USA until 1930, and sold for £200/$360 in 1988.

band with box on 14 January 1987.

The highest price paid for a foot band was £2,800/$5,040 for a set 1288, twenty-one-piece Royal Marines band with box, on 14 January 1987.

The highest price paid for a Britains Building of the 1940 series was £3,800/$6,840 for set 1748, Barracks Building, with some damage, on 29 June 1988.

The most expensive single figure ever sold at auction (at the time of writing) was the extremely

rare 70 mm single figure of the Colonel-in-Chief, the Welsh Guards, lot 109 in the Phillips sale of 9 September 1987. It was sold for £1,200/$2,160, but is known to have changed hands subsequently for a considerably higher sum.

It is interesting that in Phillips' sale of 14 February 1979, lot 238, which included one of these figures with a State Coach, was sold for a mere £55/$99, because it was wrongly described!

Chapter Four

The Shape of Collections

The basis of most smaller collections are a few items of particular interest found initially by the collector, who then proceeds to follow a definite plan of campaign, specializing in certain areas.

The majority of available toy soldiers in Britain are models of the British Army past and present, with troops of the British Empire or Commonwealth, Navy and Air Force, either in full dress for parades, or in service uniforms.

Generally, foreign troops have not been in plentiful supply, which has meant that finding an enemy side for playing youthful war-games has always proved difficult.

Small collections are usually about 500 to 2,000 figures – the amount that will comfortably fit into a single display cabinet. Medium size collections contain 2,000 to 10,000 figures, and anything more should be considered large.

By being more specialized

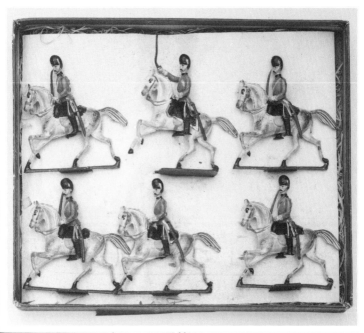

Below Courtenay two figure vignette; Sir John Keriel being defended by his squire John Fireux at the Battle of Poitiers, 1356. Courtenay knights are always made as named figures. This group sold for £180/$324 in 1981.

Below left Royal Scots Greys, 2nd Dragoons, 45mm size, German-made solid figures from about 1898; sold for £220/$396 in 1984.

small collections can be better than large collections. A collection that contains two hundred different examples of a Royal Horse Guard will be better, in that area, than many large collections. Most collectors like to follow their own inclinations in acquiring a variety of items of personal appeal, and then proceed by expanding the most interesting aspects. For instance, specialist themes might include cavalry at the halt, the British campaigns in the Sudan or plastic figures produced by Elastolin. There is an almost endless list of possibilities.

The following table provides a useful guide to the number of figures needed to form a good representative (though not exhaustive) collection. Examples of different subject areas by manufacturer and type of figure, together with the likely cost at 1989 prices and a short comment, make up the table. These

Below and right A splendid spread of Freddie Green's conversions, representing the troops of Queen Victoria to the right, and of her nephew 'Kaiser Bill' to the left. The total price of the figures in this picture was £3,200/$5,760 in 1988.

collections will allow for some duplication, enabling small parades to be mounted; some boxed and unboxed sets, some individual figures and some rarities and highlights are sufficient to make up a good and interesting display.

Because of the particular collectability of Britains figures, a separate table is provided for these on pages 80-82.

It is, of course, perfectly possible to reduce the cost of collections by buying repaired, repainted or broken figures. While, from the academic viewpoint, these are almost as good as better quality items, from the aesthetic and investment angle they are not nearly as appealing or valuable.

It is rarely possible to acquire overnight a collection as complete as that listed, unless the collection is bought lock stock and barrel from another collector. It normally

takes about five years to build up a reasonable collection of a good theme, as this involves considerable expense as well as time spent looking and buying. Putting aside £50 to £100/$90-$180 a month will enable a collection to be built up gradually.

The Shape of a Large Collection

Because toy soldiers look so good *en masse*, it is not unusal to find collections of between 10,000 and 50,000 pieces. A good-sized display of 54 mm size toy soldiers will take up about 5 cm^2 (2 in^2) per figure, so a 1.8 m x 1.2 m (6 ft x 4 ft) table can accommodate 1,500 figures of an infantry parade. Although some collectors like to feature large parades of one type, it is unusual to see more than, for

Type of Collection	Number of Figures
Flats	
Flats representing Napoleonic Troops	5,000
Flats representing First World War	2,000
Flats representing Ancient Warfare	8,000
Lucotte	
Overall collection	500
CBG Mignot	
Historical figures	1,000
Napoleonic	1,500
First World War French Army	400
Hollowcast production	2,000
Heyde	
45 mm size	
Balkan Wars	300
Armies of the World, 1910	1,000
The British Army	400
The Triumph of Germanicus	200
German made solids	
60 mm size	
Heinrich all sizes	
The British Army	300
Elastolin	
70 mm size	
The German Army 1918	500
Highlanders, all sizes	100
Lineol	
70 mm size	
Nazi personalities, SA, SS, etc.	200
British Hollowcasts other than Britains	
Pre-First World War	800
Fry, First World War	200
Johillco, full range	1,500

instance, a band and fifty other ranks; most collectors prefer to show a great variety of troops.

Collectors of Britains or Mignot have such a large range to acquire that it is easy to collect 20,000 figures without much duplication of sets. Britains figures are particularly collectable as the consistently numbered catalogues, that were issued from 1900 to 1961, make collecting examples of every numbered set a popular and by no means exhaustive interest.

Collectors of German solid figures may have a preponderance of Heyde figures, but will usually collect other makes as well. Collections of composition figures are mostly made up of Hausser and Lineol

Likely Cost	Comments
£3,000/$5,400	Not often available at auction
£800/$1,440	Not often available at auction
£6,000/$10,800	Visually exciting, vast variety
£35,000/$63,000	The most rare and expensive toy soldiers
£10,000/$18,000	Concentrates on history of France
£18,000/$36,400	Relatively common
£3,000/$5,400	Relatively inexpensive
£12,000/$21,600	Not often available outside France
£5,000/$9,000	Most attractive figures
£8,000/$14,400	Representative samples from a large range
£3,000/$5,400	The most easily acquired in the UK
£4,000/$7,200	A spectacular series of Romans
£5,000/$9,000	Includes hollowcasts
£7,000/$12,600	Attractive service dress Boxed sets rare
£1,000/$1,800	Available in UK, intricately painted
£6,000/$10,800	Expensive
£8,000/$14,400	Boxed sets rare
£1,200/$2,160	A range of about 15 sets
£5,000/$9,000	Pre-1946 boxed sets rare

products, with a few others as additions. Equally, American hollowcast 'dime store' collections concentrate on Barclay or Manoil. It is unusual to find large collections based on the products of other individual manufacturers since their output was much smaller. However, collections are often based on the products of a single country like Britain, or on a single type of manufacture, perhaps flats, solids or hollowcast figures. Today there are also many attractive large collections based almost entirely on newly-made toy-style models created with the collector in mind. After seventeen years of production, early issues of these are often rare and sought-after.

Many large collections, however, consist simply of the personal preferences of the collector. Culled from all sources,

Type of Collection	Number of Figures
Coronation Coaches, etc	500
BMC (Britannia Model Co.)	300
Timpo military models	500
Cherilea military models	200
Charbens military models	200
Crescent military models	1,000
Copies or pirates of Britains	300
Lone Star plastic models	500
Timpo plastic models	1,600
Marx unpainted plastic models	2,000
'Dime Store' figures	1,000
Quiralu aluminium figures	1,500
Wend-Al aluminium figures	500
Starlux plastic figures	2,000
Elastolin plastic figures	1,500
Authenticast and SAE 54 mm size	2,000
New toy soldiers, Sudan Campaign	2,000

Knights of Agincourt

Likely Cost	Comment
£3,000/$5,400	Coach and horses count as 9 figures (see Chapter Five)
£5,000/$9,000	The most attractive non-Britains
£2,500/$4,500	Excellent compatible range
£700/$1,260	Widely available in UK
£600/$1,080	Cheap
£2,500/$4,500	Diverse quality of figures
£2,000/$3,600	Interesting to research
£800/$1,440	Rare outside UK
£1,500/$2,700	Wide range
£3,500/$6,300	Rare outside USA
£10,000/$18,000	Rare outside USA
£10,000/$18,000	Rare outside France
£800/$1,440	Cheap
£4,000/$7,200	Excellent quality
£5,000/$9,000	The most attractive figures
£10,000/$18,000	Vast variety
£10,000/$18,000	Popular among today's subjects

part of the fun of collecting is to be able to tell the story of toy soldiers and illustrate military history, with the best (and the worst) from all manufacturers and subject areas.

In Britain, apart from Britains, other hollowcast figures are still the most widely available type. Where Britains' production is well-listed and documented, other makers were less consistent: in some cases they did not survive very long and did not always record their output. A large part of the excitement of collecting British-made hollowcasts is the frequency with which previously unseen figures come to light, particularly examples from the period before 1920. Because they were relatively cheap, these toys were not looked after carefully and so fewer survived. The vast majority of hollowcast figures on offer at swap-meets, or in antique shops, date from 1947 to 1955 and are extremely common. Prices for individual figures in good

Left Britains' medieval hollowcast figures: Set 1258 contained two tournament knights, two squires, herald and tournament marshall in their attractive illustrated box. This set should cost about £154/$270 at auction. The Knights of Agincourt were a series of five mounted and five foot figures designed by Selwyn-Smith. The mounted knights were sold individually, and cost about £40/$72 each. The foot and mounted sixteenth-century knights, lower left, were a cheap production, and are worth £2/$3.50 and £5/$9 each, respectively.

Bottom and right Collecting representations of US Army soldiers; Lucotte or Mignot 54 mm size, marching along; £130/$234; and Heyde infantry in blue coats, in action, 45 mm size £240/$432; both sold in 1984.

Below Benbros Robin Hood figures; 15 similar figures sold for £55/$99 in 1981.

condition should be in the range of £1 to £5/$1.80-$9 each; poor or broken figures are not worth collecting, except for conversion and repainting purposes.

Collecting the Extraordinary

A large part of the pleasure of collecting toy soldiers lies in the visual appeal of the models themselves. Well-made figures in the simplicity of the toy tradition are tiny works of art; armies of these form massed ranks of splendour.

Looking through the plethora of available figures, pick out the ones that appeal, and make a feature of

Below and below right Benbros hollowcast figures, British-made in the 1950s. The mounted figures are clearly copies of Britains. The foot figures are somewhat grotesque. Typical of minor British makers in the 1950s, these and eleven similar figures were sold for £25/$45 in 1981.

them by collecting a whole company, with the appropriate officers, musicians, colours, vehicles and supporting services, tents and scenery. An individual manufacturer may not provide all the required items, so it is necessary to search for similar styles made by different manufacturers. The assembly will look striking if the style is consistent throughout. Freelance designers sometimes worked on master figures for manufacturers. Wilfred Cherrington, for example, was a designer who worked for the firms of Hill, Charbens and Cherilea, among others.

Examples of Large Collections

The two most famous collections of toy soldiers ever sold at Phillips were those of Len Richards and John Hanington. Remembering that the two sales were three years apart, and that John Hanington collected more boxes and better condition figures, the varieties included in Len Richards more 'definitive' collection almost made up the difference as far as Britains figures were concerned. The catalogues of these collections are still available from Phillips, priced £5/$9 each. Here is a summary of what the collections contained.

Subject or Manufacturer	Len Richards Figures	(1981) Total Realized	John Hanington Figures	(1984) Total Realized
Britains	8,608	£53,581/$96,445	6,607	£84,479/$152,062
Hausser/Lineol	30	£265/$477	3,096	£32,970/$59,346
Mignot/Lucotte	1,220	£3,125/$5,625	1,448	£51,828/$93,290
German Solids	1,476	£3,249/$5,848	3,157	£23,701/$42,661
Flats/Semi Flats	None	——	4,103	£1,679/$3,022
British Hollowcasts	4,456	£5,080/$9,144	1,692	£2,592/$4,665
Plastics	None	——	1,060	£827/$1,488
Other toy soldiers	742	£569/$1,024	2,088	£2,222/$3,999
Militaria/Models	514	£2,793/$5,027	950	£2,977/$5,358
Total	17,046	£68,662/$123,591	24,201	£203,275/$365,895

Collecting hollowcast figures other than Britains; prices from 1981: *Below right* Early twentieth century infantry by Abel, 50 mm size, 25 similar, £55/$99; *Below* McLaughlan (US made) French Infantry, 54 mm size, 12 similar, £50/$90; *Bottom* Johillco Second World War British troops, 54 mm size, 100 similar, £90/$162.

The Forbes collection, housed chiefly at the Palais Mendoub in Tangiers, is much larger, reputedly containing 75,000 figures. A large proportion of these are flats. Numbers are not everything. Mickey's House of Soldiers in California advertises a collection of 250,000 figures to view, and the Toy Soldier Company of New York boasts a stock of 400,000 figures. To buy this quantity of figures in Esci 20 mm size plastic unpainted models, the cheaper now commercially manufactured, would take about £20,000/$36,000. From 1893 to 1966, Britains alone probably produced in excess of one thousand million hollowcast figures (a skilled operator could cast more than 300 an hour). It is a reflection on the rate of inflation that a single 20 mm size plastic unpainted model now costs ten times as much as a single Britains' best quality figure did in 1910.

Chapter Five

Royalty

The pageantry associated with royalty and heads of state brings out the best parade uniforms of the armed forces and the most spectacular displays of toy soldiers. Models of royalty and their immediate attendants, state coaches and body guards are sufficiently common to make an interesting collection, acquired without too much difficulty. Britains Yeomen of the Guard, for instance, are available at about £6 to £10/$11-$18 each; by other

makers in good qualities at between £3 and £5/$5-$9 each; or in poor quality at between £1 and £3/$1.80-$5. European manufacturers sometimes made examples of the famous Yeoman for the British market, and these would be more expensive.

State coaches are a subject sought by collectors of royal memorabilia; as is typical with any collecting field, there are associations and overlaps into other fields. A collector of state

Left Britains set 2081, the largest sold after the Second World War, and the second largest ever made, contained 228 figures. On offer only in 1953, the set featured the State Coach, Attendants, Sovereign's Standard and Escort, Life Guards, Horse Guards, Irish Guards and Royal Marines. Everything in the set was available in smaller sets, except for the officers of the Horse Guards, with the base painted brown to match the other bases in the set. In the regular set of Horse Guards, set 2, the base is painted green.

Manufacturer	Approx overall length	Monarch	Start of Manufacture
Timpo	45 cm	Elizabeth II	1953
Britains	38 cm	Edward VIII	1937
Britians	38 cm	George VI	1937
Britains	38 cm	Elizabeth II	1953
Heyde	35 cm	George V	1910
Lesney	30 cm	George VI	1952
Lesney	30 cm	Elizabeth II	1953
Johillco	28 cm	George V	1935
Johillco	28 cm	George VI	1937
Johillco	28 cm	Elizabeth II	1953
Crescent	25 cm	Elizabeth II	1953
Crescent	25 cm	Elizabeth II	1978
Britains	20 cm	George VI	1937
Britains	20 cm	Elizabeth II	1953
Barrett	18 cm	Elizabeth II	1953
Benbros	13 cm	Elizabeth II	1953
Lesney	13 cm	Elizabeth II	1953

Approx Value	Attendants Available	Display Boxes
£200/$360	Yes	Yes
£1,500/$2,700	Yes	No
£200/$360	Yes	Yes
£200/$360	Yes	Yes
£400/$720	Yes	Yes
£100/$180	No	No
£75/$135	No	No
£60/$108	Yes	Yes
£50/$90	Yes	Yes
£40/$72	Yes	Yes
£30/$54	Yes	Yes
£15/$27	Yes	Yes
£35/$63	No	No
£25/$45	No	No
£20/$36	No	No
£15/$27	No	No
£15/$27	No	No

Below Heyde State Coach. This fine 45 mm size state coach is obviously not a model of the State Coach of England, but the figures and horses with it are certainly of British personalities and attendants. A possible guess might be that this represents Edward Prince of Wales and his wife Alexandra in their coach, at the Diamond Jubilee of his mother Queen Victoria in 1898. It was sold at Phillips, in 1984, for £240/$432.

Below Mounted figure of Henry V, by Courtenay.

coaches might pursue his interest from the point of view of a toy soldier collector, since the majority of state coach models have been made by manufacturers who also made toy soldiers: hence the British state coach has been made by Britains, Johillco, Crescent, Taylor and Timpo. Other manufacturers of the state coach, such as Lesney and Benbros, were primarily die-cast vehicle makers. Even tin toy or biscuit tin manufacturers produced state coaches.

The real state coach actually began its life as a model, produced soon after it was originally commissioned. The model, still in the possession of the Coach Makers and Coach Harness Makers Company, was designed by Sir William Chambers, carved by Wilton with the panels painted by Cipriani. This model was constructed before building the full size coach actually began, in 1762.

The most famous state coach in toy collecting is the large Lesney coach, which is about 30 cm long. It was first made in 1952, and in about 1968 someone put an advertisement in the London *Times* Personal Column offering to pay £100/$180 for an example. For a year thereafter, the column was full of people trying to sell these coaches at similar prices. This was just the period when it was becoming fashionable to collect toys. The advertisements for state coaches made such an impression on the minds of the public that state coaches became widely known as 'expensive', and there is still a tendency for people to bring them to auction with high expectations. In fact, very good boxed examples of the large Lesney coach did not reach £100/$180 in 1988, and for many years it was possible to buy one for £20/

$36. Yet there are still some who insist that the *small* Lesney coach, almost 11 cm long 'was worth £100 twenty years ago and must be worth a fortune today'!

Toy state coaches were often available with the attendants to the coach: nine outriders, six footmen and four Yeomen of the Guard, who walk alongside the State Coach of England on ceremonial occasions. Sometimes large display boxes, with combined coaches and attendants or with the addition of guards and police, were produced. 1989 values are for examples in excellent condition and in their original boxes.

Because these souvenir coaches were extremely popular, they are now relatively easy to collect, and there are many other souvenir models: royal figures in coronation robes, thrones and other types of coach such as the state landau. Because Edward VIII was never crowned, items prepared as souvenirs of his forthcoming coronation were quickly withdrawn and, consequently, are particularly rare and very sought-after. The

Left Colonel-in-Chief, the Welsh Guards, in 70 mm size. This figure was first produced as a souvenir figure of Edward Prince of Wales for Madame Tussauds in the late 1930s, but appears here as a souvenir of the royal visit to South Africa in 1947. It was sold at Phillips, in September 1987, for £1,200/ $2,160, currently a record for a single toy soldier.

Below left Mounted figure in 120 mm size – very similar to the above picture – and a souvenir figure of the Prince of Wales, but made in Germany, probably by Heyde. Sold for £240/$432 in 1988.

Below So many toy soldiers can be connected to royalty. This Royal Navy gun carriage is of the sort that could be used as the funeral bier for a king. This gun carriage only appeared in set 131, and is a Royal Horse Artillery limber with wires attached. The naval ratings are soldered to the wire.

most splendid item to be acquired is the 228-piece set made by Britains for the coronation of Elizabeth II. A nearly complete example of this set was sold by Phillips in 1987 for £3,000/$5,400, after being sold at Christie's in 1981 for only £480/$864. This is symptomatic of the recent interest among collectors in large sets and boxes.

Right Cherilea figures: the Black Prince and Richard Lionhart. The former is very rare and worth £30$54.

Below right Heads of state can also be added to the Royal Collection. Here, French-made figures of Napoleon and George Washington, by Carman.

Below An extremely rare Britains figure of the Emperor of Germany. This sold for £100/$180 in 1980. *(Sotheby's).*

Chapter Six

Britains
– The World's Favourite Toy Soldiers

William Britain was a nineteenth-century toy manufacturer who ran a family business making and selling good quality mechanical toys. His son, William Britain Jr, is credited with developing the hollowcasting process for making toy soldiers, and the first hollowcast Britains sets came on the market in 1893.

Successful production of toy soldiers has been continuous from 1893 right through to the present day, with Britains' products being consistently favoured above all others by the majority of the world's collectors. Hollowcast production has been superseded by plastic and die-cast models, but there are echoes of the past even in the latest products.

By 1898, Britains' range was sufficiently extensive to merit a numbering system that enabled retailers to order the various sets. Numbers were rigorously applied to packaging as well as to lists and catalogues issued. Over 144 editions of the Britains Toy Soldier List are reputed to have been issued; these form the basis for collectors to research missing sets to add to their collections.

Britains were also always concerned to improve their toys, and many changes of design and

Below and bottom Territorial Infantry in red or blue coats were made for the Coronation of George V in 1910. These, among the rarest of Britains figures, were sold at Phillips in 1988 for a total of £8,100/ $14,580, an average of £540/$972 per figure. The Spanish Infantry were made on the occasion of the Cuban War in 1898. The previous set, depicted the opposing US Infantry. Both sets were made from a British Infantryman with a new head. This set, in spite of having arms missing and rifles damaged, sold for £650/$1,170 in 1988.

Below Britains' boxes were most attractive. Usually deep red, they had labels either typographical, decorated, designed by Fred Whisstock, or standard with titles printed later. One of the fascinations of collecting Britains is to find as many different box labels as possible for a single set.

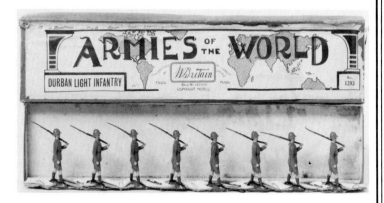

Below The Durban Light Infantry are very similar in appearance to set 1294, British Infantry in Tropical Service Dress. The box itself is often the only way to tell the two apart.

style were made over the years.

Because they retained the same catalogue numbering system for so long, the changes Britains made are particularly interesting: each set has a discernible series of variations that conform to the overall pattern of manufacture and development.

Britains' hollowcast toy soldier manufacturing period (1893-1966) can be conveniently split into three eras because manufacturing had to be stopped during the two World Wars. Production was resumed after both wars with quite a number of variations. Each era breaks down into two periods.

ERA 1
BEFORE THE FIRST
WORLD WAR
First Period:
Early expansion, 1893-1900 (sets started, 1 to 103). Figures were mainly fixed-arm models and had oval bases. No identifying lettering appeared anywhere on figures. Frequent improvement to

figures was made. Box labels were illustrated or of a plain type with printers' decorations and were not numbered until 1898.
Second Period:
Dated production, 1900-1916 (sets started, 104 to 197). All figures were identified with either paper labels or with moulded lettering, and included the date that the master figure was copyrighted. In 1911 the law was changed so that the date was no longer needed on the figures; over the next fifteen years Britains phased out the models with dates. From about 1910, the artist Fred Whisstock was employed to design a wide range of box labels.

ERA 2
BETWEEN THE WARS
First Period:
Consolidation, 1919-1932 (sets started, 198 to 500). The range gradually increased, with more effort being made to develop non-military lines such as the 'Home Farm' series. Many new set-

Left One figure painted as a number of different regiments did duty as the mounted troops of the British Indian Empire. This is a beautiful double row display box of Hodsons Horse, worth about £500/ $900. In the single row set 46, either the officer or the trumpeter would appear. In the double row set 63, both would feature.

Bottom The Middlesex Regiment, set 76, appeared for a short time at the trail, using the 'wasp-waisted' figure. Although there is one figure missing, this beautiful boxed set fetched £1,400/$2,520 at Phillips, in 1988.

numbers in fact denoted the new packaging of existing figures. Major export drives to North and South America were begun. Box labels (until set 400) continued to be designed by Fred Whisstock. Numbers 501 to 1200 in the catalogue listing were used for non-military individual figures, such as farm animals; military numbers resumed at 1201.

Second Period:
Proliferation, 1932-41 (sets started, 1201 to 1920). The range was greatly increased, partly for export. Events leading to many new issues included the 1937 coronation of King George VI and the re-armament drive from 1936 onwards as a counter to Nazi Germany. The latter event was reflected by the introduction of toys depicting battle-dress troops and vehicles and the equipment

for air-raid precautions. Whisstock-designed labels were gradually superseded by a new range of standard or illustrated labels.

ERA 3
AFTER THE SECOND WORLD WAR
First Period:
Recovery, 1946-55 (sets started, 2001-2117). Production was re-started with a limited number of existing sets, mostly for export. The range was then built up gradually with the addition of some new sets. There were no moustaches painted on figures from 1940 onwards. Labels were completely standardized to 'Regiments of All Nations' for military subjects. But, old labels continued to be issued until supplies ran out – for some sets as late as 1954.

Second Period:
Decline, 1956-1966 (sets started, 2118 to 2189). Plastic moulded toy soldiers spelt the death of hollowcasting, and after 1955 all firms other than Britains were quickly forced out of hollowcasting production. Britains continued to produce metal figures as an expensive prestige line, and new packaging and selling methods – 'picture packs', smaller sets and window boxes – were used to try to increase the firm's sales. It was a losing battle – the last few sets were produced for export in 1966.

Plastic Production

Britains' essay at producing plastic toy soldiers began in 1954 when they marketed the Herald range of plastic figures prior to taking over that firm. Herald figures are arguably the best-

sculpted toy soldiers ever made. Later on, though, these figures were issued in a cheap edition, moulded in an inferior plastic in Hong Kong.

Britains then pioneered the creation of the 'Swoppet', the plastic figure with interchangeable parts and movable head and waist, the forerunner of hundreds of similar action-figures and culminating in the space fantasy characters popular today.

Much more reminiscent of the hollowcast range were the 'Eyes Right' series of full-dress troops, which had movable arms and turnable plug-in heads. The bandsmen had metal instruments plated in chrome or brass, and these figures are also very highly esteemed by collectors. A household cavalry figure was produced following, almost

Below An assortment of early Britains boxes. The earliest is that for set 3, *top right*. The figures on view are the Boer Cavalry and Boer Infantry, both sets are quite likely to cost £1,000/$1,800 with their boxes. *(Sotheby's)*

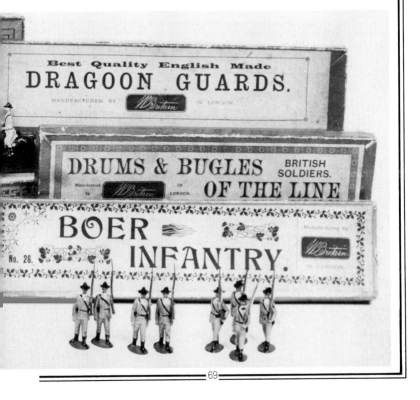

exactly, the standard hollowcast figure.

More recently, a new range of plastic figures called the Deetail range has been introduced. This in itself has now had a twenty-year life. All figures in the range have die-cast metal bases, which overcomes the problem of plastic figures toppling over easily because they are so light.

All these figures, except the most recent Deetail issues, are already highly collectable.

New Metal Models

In 1973 Britains produced an experimental die-cast metal Foot Guard, and some years later, in 1982, it was decided to expand the die-cast metal range. These figures are now produced in small quantities for the souvenir, collector and toy markets; they thus fall between the new toy soldier and the old in terms of purpose of manufacture. Limited-edition sets have been produced with collectors in mind, with a better quality paint and finish than the standard issue. Since the basic figures of this new series cost between £1 and £2/$1.80-$3.60 each, many collectors use them as the basis for conversions.

Collecting Britains by Catalogue Number

At first glance it would seem an easy matter to collect Britains toy soldiers by simply starting at set 1 and obtaining an example of each set in the best quality range military series. These sets run from 1 to 500, 1,201 to 1,919 and 2,001 to 2,189, a total of 1,407 numbers.

Many sets, however, were simply reissues of already existing figures in new sizes or combinations of packaging. Although a complete collection of Britains would include an example

Left and below Paris office figures: Britains exported to France and opened a Paris office. From 1912 to 1923, this office had its own factory painting and casting figures never made in England. They are rare, and include many interesting features such as standard bearers. Good examples of individual figures are worth between £50-£200/$90-$360 each.

of every set, the amount of duplication is so very large that, in practice, few collectors attempt it. To attempt such a collection would be made difficult by the scarcity of other than standard-size sets.

There is evidence that some numbers were never used, probably because they were provisionally allocated to sets that never saw the light of day. These form a small proportion – only 23 being unaccounted for. More common are those sets which, although the title is known, were never introduced in the general catalogue, and may therefore have been orders for very specialized markets.

The upshot of this is that instead of 1,407 numbers, there are actually only about 600, excluding combination sets, repetitions with small differences, some civilian sets that appeared in the main military series and cowboys and Indians, as well as the sets which

Right The Boer Cavalry was also used for the African Mounted Police.

Below and right The Lancer officer, turned in the saddle, is one of Britains' most delightful figures – here is a front and back view. The figure of a 9th Lancer is worth about £25/$45.

never appeared in the catalogue.

This reduced complement is possible to achieve, but leaves out the other collecting possibilities. Second grade and small-size figures had their own series of catalogue numbers. Some large sets contained figures unobtainable in a standard set. Nor does the acquisition of a single set take account of the various versions in which that set might have been sold. There are, therefore, no straightforward criteria to be applied to collecting Britains figures!

The more popular the regiment, the more variations Britains would produce, both in the style of figure and in the versions of improvement the figure underwent. The Household Cavalry, for instance, was produced with 51 different Life Guards and 38 different Horse Guards, quite apart from variations in paint style. The Foot Guards were the most numerous of the infantry types, although they were never issued on guard. Line Infantry were issued in a very large number of sets, but never as a colour party. Scots Greys were the most popular cavalry after the Household, and were the only other regiment to be issued with a mounted band. Fusiliers were popular, but were only issued

Below left Britains set 2014, the Band of the US Marine Corps; winter dress. This band was introduced soon after the Second World War as part of Britains' export drive to the USA. It proved quite popular, but not all that many sets have survived, and it is worth up to £2,000/$3,600 in 1989. The box looks enormous compared to the band, which was well spread out when tied inside. The label is the standard style for the period 1950-61; nearly all Britains' boxes could be recognized by their distinctive red colour.

Below A large group of Britains' specially painted Cameron Highlanders, 1956 vintage. These were never issued as numbered sets.

marching at the slope, except for a brief period in the 1950s when they were shown at attention.

In Britain, officers, drummers and standard bearers were hardly ever issued in quantities comparable to those produced by European manufacturers, who included them in sets. The Paris office, set up by Britains to sell models in France, eventually manufactured its own figures, presumably partly to rival the Mignot sets which usually included officers, drummers and standard bearers.

Picture packs were individually boxed best quality figures marketed from 1955 to 1958. Britains had hitherto concentrated on selling sets only, although second grade troops were available loose and some early attempts at counter-packs of loose figures had been made before the First World War. Woolworths, who under their policy of threepenny and sixpenny sales lines could not afford to sell Britains' boxed sets, used to take the best quality soldiers out of the boxes and sell them individually at threepence each in the 1930s.

Above This box of 'Germanic' Royal Fusiliers, typical of Britains' extremely early boxes, still holds the price record for a single-row box, at £3,500/$6,300 in 1984. The officer is mounted on the same horse as the set of Scots Greys, which is equally rare. Neither were ever issued as a numbered set.

Left Zulu Kraal. An extra hut is included, and the Zulus' shields are repainted. In spite of this, this rare scenic box fetched £480/$864 in 1984. More recently, in 1988, a better example fetched £800/$1,440.

List of Collecting Subjects for Britains Ltd.

The listing gives the number of figures or items that it would take to form a good (though not exhaustive) collection of the subject. This includes examples of some different versions of sequences, some boxed sets and some rarities. Some collectors prefer to collect Britains by set number only, but this in no way covers the full output since, when requested, Britains would also produce figures painted or cast to order. Naturally, these cost more than the standard range and, much sought-after today, they are known as 'Britains Specials'. Any non-standard paint or casting painted in Britains' normal or slightly rarer style may well be a 'Britains Special'. But these are not common, and it is as well to be careful that such figures are not simply well-made conversions or repaintings.

Below Britains Toytown figures. A prototype for a set never issued on the open market, these figures were invented uniforms, painted by a mechanical process rather than by hand. This possibly unique set fetched £2,200/$3,960 in 1987.

COLLECTING SUBJECTS: BRITAINS LTD

Figures of British Types	Number of Figures	Likely Cost
1. Royalty, bodyguards and general staff	200	£3,000/$5,400
2. Household cavalry	300	£6,000/$10,800
3. Foot Guards	1,000	£15,000/$27,000
4. Dragoon Guards and Dragoons	100	£4,000/$7,200
5. Hussars	150	£6,000/$10,800
6. Lancers	150	£7,000/$12,600
7. Infantry of the line	600	£10,000/$18,000
8. Scottish regiments	500	£10,000/$18,000
9. Other full-dress infantry	150	£6,000/$10,800
10. Royal Artillery	200	£20,000/$36,000
11. Royal Navy and Marines	300	£8,000/$14,400
12. Auxiliary Services	150	£6,000/$10,800
13. The Boer War	150	£6,000/$10,800
14. British Army in khaki	400	£4,000/$7,200
15. Motor vehicles	50	£3,000/$5,400

Figures of Empire and Foreign Types

	Number of Figures	Likely Cost
16. The Indian Empire	150	£6,000/$10,800
17. Canada	120	£3,000/$5,400
18. Rest of the British Empire	150	£4,000/$7,200
19. France	200	£6,000/$10,800
20. Europe	200	£10,000/$18,000
21. Asia and Africa	100	£3,000/$5,400
22. United States of America	250	£6,000/$10,800
23. Latin America	100	£5,000/$9,000

Other Types

	Number of Figures	Likely Cost
24. Historical items (pre-1870)	100	£2,000/$3,600
25. Cowboys, Indians and American Civil War	200	£1,500/$2,700
26. Military buildings	10	£10,000/$18,000
27. Police and uniformed civilians	100	£3,000/$5,400
28. Picture packs	100	£2,000/$3,600
29. Small-size types	250	£4,000/$7,200
30. Second grade types	400	£1,500/$2,700
31. Royal Air Force	50	£5,000/$9,000
32. Models of guns	50	£1,000/$1,800

Most sought after
Sets

Gentlemen at arms
Early mounted bands
Slotted arm band

Dismounted Scots Grey
Middlesex Yeomanry
Plug shoulder lancers
Regiments of the
British Army
Cameronians
Berkshire Regiment Band
Steel-helmeted gun team
Royal Marine Light
Infantry Band
Pontoon wagon,
collar harness
Army service supply
column
Infantry at ease,
First version
Round bonnet
under-slung, long

Full-dress Mountain
Artillery
Lord Strathcona's Horse
Bahamas Police Band
Paris office figures
Greek Cavalry
Zulu Kraal
Marines, service dress
Argentine Cadets,
peak caps

Knights of Agincourt

Large boxed sets

Parade ground with
barracks
Salvation Army
Cavalry standards
Russian Cavalry
Early sets
Aircraft
4.5 in. anti-aircraft gun

33.	Farm	500	£5,000/$9,000
34.	Zoo	200	£3,000/$5,400
35.	Garden	500	£1,500/$2,700
36.	Other civilians	200	£3,500/$6,300
37.	Novelties	50	£1,500/$2,700
38.	Eyes Right models	400	£2,000/$3,600
39.	Other plastic toy soldiers	1,000	£2,000/$3,600
40.	New metal toy soldiers	300	£700/$1,260

Total, for a reasonably comprehensive collection of Britains products

£206,200/$371,160

Village idiot, buildings
Rubber-nosed
elephant, buildings
Garden-shelter,
boxed sets
Motor cycle and side-car
Early automata
US Bands
English Civil War
Highlanders, limited
edition sets

By way of comparison with what might be a near complete or major collection of Britains, £20,000/ $36,000 is allocated for Royal Artillery. The case study in the next chapter gives horse-drawn gun teams from these subject areas, with a total value approaching £50,000/$90,000 for a collection that includes just one example of each variation.

Far left Set 2017, Ski-troops, attractive figures first made soon after the Second World War. A set of four with its original box is worth £400/$720.

Left Set 2013 was made as a twelve piece display of Indian Army cavalry, to commemorate Indian Independence. The set was never offered in the catalogue, and is extremely rare, worth about £1,200/$2,160.

Chapter Seven

Case Study:
Britains Horse Drawn Vehicles

By way of an example of building up a detailed collection of Britains, this chapter surveys one subject in particular: that of military horse-drawn vehicles. This is just one of the many specialist fields in Britains' output. Some of the collecting areas overlap, but to concentrate on one will give an idea of the complexity specialist collecting can entail. Horse-drawn vehicles come from the Royal Artillery and Auxiliary Services subject areas, and Britains made just four vehicles:

Limber (3 versions with 3 additional variations)

General Purpose Wagon (2 versions)
Great Purpose Limbered Wagon (1 version)
Pontoon Wagon (1 version)

Set 39, the Royal Horse Artillery, was first made in 1895, and it was not until 1906 that Britains brought out a wider range of horse-drawn items. Over the course of production from 1906 to 1966, the date that an item was produced can be narrowed down by noticing details of the wire harness, the colour of the vehicle, the type of horse, the moustaches on the men and the type of seated

Royal Horse Artillery at the Gallop
– Set 39

Version	Variations	Date
1 Shafted Limber	None – heavy twisted wire	1895-1906
2 Centre Pole Limber	Grey paint, twisted wire	1906-1912
	Khaki paint (matt)	1913-1916
	Fumed metal, open-spring gun	1919-1924
3 Light Harness	Fumed metal	1924-1932
4 Rear Opening		
Limber	Mid-khaki paint	1932-1936
	Dark-green	1936-1939
	Mid-khaki, no moustaches	1939-1942
5 Wire Clip Traces	Dark-green, larger limber wheels	1948-1958
	Matt-green paint	1959-1966

man. When there are major changes in the model, these are termed versions. When there are minor changes, these are termed variations. The difference between the two categories is not always clear, and sometimes several variations combined would be termed a new version. By consensus the sets produced after the Second World War are held to be new versions, even though their difference from pre-war versions is sometimes apparent only in the style of painting. The following table lists the versions and variations for set 39:

Left First version collar harness gun team with shafted limber and seated gunners. Probably the favourite of all Britains gun teams among collectors, one excellent example with box has been sold for £3,000/$5,400, but normally, since this version was only made before 1906, there are defects, and consequently, prices are lower.

These are the five versions of the R.H.A., with five variations based on the paint finish. Additional variations, based on the changes in the mounted officer and outriders, could also be included. Version 1 had four gunners on bucket seats, whereas from 1906 these gunners were mounted on horses and included in an enlarged box.

Individual changes to all the variables are shown below:

| Changes to team horses: | Collar harness (galloping and walking only) | 1895-1924 |
| | Breast harness (also known as light harness) | 1924-1966 |

The team horse at the halt was introduced in 1929. Total: five different horses, each in pairs, mounted and unmounted.

Changes to wire traces:	Twisted wire traces (heavier gauge before 1906)	1895-1916
	Thin wire traces	1919-1948
	Wire-clip traces	1948-1966
Changes to seated men:	First version with moulded cross-belt	1906-1916
	Second version with larger head	1919-1965

The limber was used in the artillery gun-team sets. The first limber, made in 1895, was called the shafted limber, as it incorporated shafts for the unridden team horse immediately in front of it.

Changes to Limber:	Shafted limber	1895-1906
	Centre-pole limber, no seat slots	1906-1932
	Centre-pole limber, seat slots	1906-1924
	Rear-opening limber	1932-1948
	Rear-opening limber with wire clips	1948-1966

Right The gun team at the halt, in sevice dress, set 318, was sold with a crew of eight gunners and a mounted officer. This example sold at Phillips for £6,500/$11,700 in 1987.

The centre-pole limber with seat slots was used for Royal Field Artillery sets with seated gunners. The change simply involved a different casting of the limber lid.

Changes to Royal Artillery Gun:

R.A. Gun with bucket seats	1895-1916
R.A. Gun without bucket seats	1895-1916
R.A. Gun with open trail	1919-1932
R.A. Gun no. 1201, small wheels	1932-1948
R.A. Gun no. 1201, large wheels	1948-1966

The Royal Horse Artillery used the R.A. gun with bucket seats from 1895 to 1906, when the seated gunners were given horses. The Royal Field Artillery used the R.A. gun with bucket seats from 1906 to 1916. The R.A. gun *without* bucket seats was available separately before it was used with an artillery team.

Changes to vehicle paint finish:

Semi-matt grey	*c.* 1895-1912
Semi-matt khaki	*c.* 1912-1916
Fumed-metal finish	1919-1932
Mid-khaki gloss	1932-1936
	and *c.* 1940-1952
Dark green gloss	1936-1939
	and *c.* 1952-1958
Matt dull green	1959-1966

The periods approximated above have not been exactly determined, although the dates shown seem likely. Guns were painted in the same colours, but the R.A. gun had a bronze barrel until 1919.

As is the case with the rest of Britains British Army figures: before 1939 all human faces had painted moustaches; after 1939 they did not.

Mismatched sets can be detected in the wiring attached to the team horses. If the style of wiring does not match the period of the limber or the normal gauge of wire used by Britains, it is suspect. And it is worth noting that the mounted team horse is *always* positioned to the left of the riderless team horse.

Horse-drawn vehicles are very liable to damage, and are often found in a battered or repaired state. It is important to notice whether horses hooves, legs or tails are missing, and if the drivers' whips are intact; helmet furniture, either spikes or balls, break off easily, as do the plumes and cap-lines from the busbys of the Royal Horse Artillery. Wire traces should all be present and should match; vehicles should have all rails and hinged parts complete; limbers should ideally contain a full complement of ammunition for the gun.

Repairs can often be detected by carefully checking the horses in the team against each other, comparing the size of legs and tails and the colour of the paint. Drivers' heads should also be checked against each other. Recast or mismatched seated men are also commonly found: recast men will be too heavy, the paintwork often incorrect.

A good, original first-version set 39 Royal Horse Artillery team, in its box, can be worth £3,000/$5,400, while a damaged or repaired example may only be worth £150/$270. The significant difference in value shows how important it is to check each figure for damage and signs of repairs.

The four basic vehicles produced by Britains were sold in the various guises listed. Included in the list are the prices likely to be reached by such items at an auction today. The date of manufacture enables specific versions to be determined. The limber was made into gun teams:

Left This steel-helmeted Band of the US Army in 1940 uniform sold for £2,100/$3,780 in 1988. The figures at the back, including the USA Infantry 'Doughboy' figure in a steel helmet, are also rare.

Set		Date of Manufacture	Value
	Royal Horse Artillery, Gallop		
39	With bucket seats	1900	£2,000/$3,600
39	With mounted gunners	1910	£800/$1,440
39	With breast harness	1930	£400/$720
39	With late-version gun	1960	£300/$540
39A	With service dress	1916	£2,000/$3,600
1339	With breast harness	1930	£800/$1,440
1339	With steel helmets	1940	£6,000/$10,800
	Royal Field Artillery, Walk		
144	With bucket seats	1910	£2,000/$3,600
144	With breast harness	1930	£700/$1,260
144	With late-version gun	1935	£600/$1,080
144A	With service dress	1916	£1,200/$2,160
144A	With breast harness	1930	£800/$1,440
1440	With late-version gun	1935	£600/$1,080
1440	With steel helmets	1940	£6,000/$10,800
	Royal Artillery with 46 cm (18 in) Howitzer, Walk		
211	With breast harness	1925	£1,000/$1,800
	Royal Horse Artillery, Halt		
316	With early-version gun	1929	£2,500/$4,500
316	With late-version gun	1935	£2,000/$3,600
	Royal Field Artillery, Halt		
317	With early-version gun	1929	£3,000/$5,400
317	With later-version gun	1935	£2,500/$4,500
318	With service dress	1929	£3,500/$6,300
318	With late-version gun	1935	£2,500/$4,500
318	With steel helmets	1940	£7,000/$12,600
	Royal Horse Artillery, Walk		
2077	With late-version gun	1955	£400/$720
		Total:	£48,600/$87,480

Below The St John's Series was presumably made up for a wholesaler by Britains, since no trade mark or set number appears on the box. The figures are all Britains. The set sold for £800/$1,440 in 1984.

The General Service Wagon was made up into the Royal Army Medical Corps four-horse ambulance, and the Royal Army Service Corps two-horse supply wagon. It is also known to have been made up into various European military wagons by Britains' Paris Office, and into U.S. Army vehicles. But, more famously, it was produced as a two-wagon-with-escort set, distributed by a firm with the initials C.F.E., and entitled Army Supply Column, the figures complete with slouch hats.

Set		Date of Manufacture	Value
	RAMC Ambulance		
145	Collar harness	1910	£400/$720
145	Breast harness	1935	£300/$540
145	Late-version wagon	1955	£300/$540
145A	Service dress	1916	£500/$900
1450	Breast harness	1935	£400/$720
1450	Steel helmets	1940	£3,000/$5,400
	RASC Supply Wagon		
146	Collar harness	1910	£250/$450
146	Breast harness	1935	£200/$360
146	Late-version wagon	1955	£200/$360
145A	Service dress	1916	£300/$540
1450	Breast harness	1935	£250/$450
1450	Steel helmets	1940	£2,500/$4,500
	Army Supply Column		
No number	Collar harness	1910	£5,000/$9,000
	US Army Wagons*		
1371	Two-horse wagon, peak caps	1934	£2,000/$3,600
1371	Steel helmets	1940	£3,000/$5,400
1372	Four-horse ambulance, peak caps	1934	£2,500/$4,500
1372	Steel helmets	1940	£4,000/$7,200
	Paris Office Wagon		
No number	French – two-horse	1915	£3,000/$5,400

*The prices for these vehicles are conjectural since they are so rare that they have not appeared at auction in recent years.

The Pontoon wagon was used simply for set 203 Pontoon Section, a four-horse boat wagon with boat and two roadway sections, its khaki service-dress equivalent, set 1254, and the US set 1373. The steel-helmeted versions of these latter two sets are assumed to have existed, but no authentic example has ever appeared at auction.

Set		Date of Manufacture	Value
	Pontoon Section		
	Royal Engineers		
203	Collar harness	1922	£1,200/$2,160
203	Breast harness	1935	£800/$1,440
1254	Khaki service dress	1935	£1,000/$1,800
1254	Steel-helmeted	1940	£5,000/$9,000
1373	US Army Engineers		
	Military Bridging		
	Section	1934	£3,000/$5,400
1373	Steel-helmeted	1940	£6,000/$10,800

The Limbered General Service Wagon appeared under the same set numbers with galloping or walking horses.

Set		Date of Manufacture	Value
1329	Royal Army Service		
	Corps, walking horses	1935	£650/$1,170
1329	Galloping horses	1935	£850/$1,530
1330	Royal Engineers,		
	walking horses	1935	£400/$720
1330	Galloping horses	1933	£400/$720
1330	Post-war version,		
	walking horses	1955	£400/$720
1330	Galloping horses	1955	£300/$540
1331	Service dress,		
	walking horses	1935	£600/$1,080
1331	Galloping horses	1935	£800/$1,440
1331	Steel-helmeted,		
	walking horses	1940	£2,500/$4,500
1331	Galloping horses	1940	£3,000/$5,400

Above Britains set 1339, Royal Horse Artillery Gun Team, service dress with steel helmets. The mounted gunners are on the pre-World War II style horse, as opposed to the similar post-World War II set where the gunners are mounted on horses with fully outstretched legs. This set sold for £7,000/$12,600 in 1987.

Left Infantry at ease with service dress and steel helmets: the first version of set 1828 and extremely rare. The complete set sold for £190/$342, probably worth £700/$1,260 in 1989.

Below Royal Artillery Gun teams at the halt: set 316, Royal Horse Artillery, on the right, sold for £2,000/$3,600 in 1984; set 317, Field Artillery, sold for £2,200/$3,960 in the same sale.

The Mystique of the Steel Helmets

In late 1939-1940, Britains decided to put steel helmets onto all their service dress horse-drawn vehicle drivers and seated men, replacing the peak caps with which they had previously been equipped. This may have been a direct response to the outbreak of the Second World War. As production stopped in 1941, and most production in the course of the two years before had been limited, these steel-helmeted sets are now extremely rare. A few may have been issued for sale in 1945 after the War ended.

The variety of these versions of the horse-drawn vehicle, in what is one of the most popular collecting areas, makes them probably the most sought-after item in the toy soldier collecting market. Yet, the only intrinsic difference between them and normal service-dress vehicles is the change of heads; this makes them relatively easy to fake.

There are other examples of khaki service-dress sets that were given steel helmets. These include some sets of United States Army troops issued with British-style steel helmets (as worn by the US Army at this period), but these sets appear so rarely that they may only have been issued as specials, samples or export orders.

By contrast, the British Infantry in steel helmets (set 195 and its various successors) are common and inexpensive. A very good set of seven men and an officer, in original box, may cost no more than £60/$108. Individual examples in fair condition may cost £2 or £3/$3.60-$5 each. Fixed-arm infantry in battle dress from the Second World War are even cheaper; machine gunners, available in peak caps and steel helmets, are also inexpensive.

Right Gun teams also made spectacular conversions. This Belgian Horse Artillery Team was converted from Britains by Freddie Green, and sold for £150/$270 in 1988.

Right and below Horse-drawn vehicles, riders in steel helmets: Gun teams at the halt, sold for £3,000/$5,400 in 1988; Ambulance sold for £4,000/$7,200 in 1986; Limbered wagon, at the walk, sold for £3,500/$6,300 in 1986.

Bibliography

Allendesalazar, J. M., *Colleccionissimo de Soldades* (Editorial Everest, Spain, 1978)

Baldet, Marcel, *Figurines et Soldats de Plomb* (Paris 1961)

Carmen, W. Y., *Model Soldiers* (Charles Letts, 1973)

Garratt, John G., *Model Soldiers, a Collector's Guide* (Seeley Service, 1965)

Garratt, John G., *The World Encyclopedia of Model Soldiers* (Muller, 1981)

Kurtz, Henry I. and Ehrlich, Burtt R., *The Art of the Toy Soldier* (New Cavendish, 1979)

Polaine, Reggie, *The War Toys No 1: The Story of Hausser-Elastolin* (New Cavendish, 1979)

Formana, Dennis, *The War Toys No 2: The Story of Lineol* (In preparation)

Johnson, Peter, *Toy Armies* (Batsford, 1982)

McKenzie, Ian, *Collecting Old Toy Soldiers* (Batsford, 1975)

Gardiner, Gordon and Morris, Alistair, *Metal Toys* (Salamander, 1984)

O'Brien, Richard, *Collecting Toy Soldiers* (Private publication, 1988)

O'Brein, Richard, *The Barclay Catalogue Book* (Private publication)

Opie, James, *Toy Soldiers* (Shire, 1983)

Opie, James, *British Toy Soldiers 1893 to the Present* (Arms & Armour Press, 1985)

Opie, James, *Britains Toy Soldiers 1893-1932* (Gollancz, 1985)

Opie, James, *Collecting Toy Soldiers* (Collins, 1987)

Rose, Andrew, *The Collectors All Colour Guide to Toy Soldiers* (Salamander, 1985)

Ortmann, Erwin, *Model Tin Soldiers* (Studio Vista, 1974)

Richards, L. W., *Old British Model Soldiers, 1893-1918* (Arms & Armour Press, 1970)

Roer, Hans H., *Bleisoldaten* (Callwey, 1981)

Ruddell, Joanne and Ron, *The Britains Collectors Checklist* (Private publication)

Ruddle, John *A Collectors Guide to Britains Model Soldiers* (Model & Allied Publications, 1980)

Wally, Joe, *Regiments of All Nations* (Private publication)

Magazines

Bulletin of the British Model Soldier Society, J. Cox, Membership Secretary, 6 Anderson Close, Woodley, Romsey, Hampshire SO5 17UE

Military Hobbies, A. E. Morgan Publications Ltd, Stanley House, 9 West Street, Epsom, Surrey KT18 9RL

Old Toy Soldier Newletter, 209 North Lombard, Oak Park, Illinois 60302, USA

The Plastic Warrior, 65 Walton Court, Woking, Surrey GU21 5EE

Toy Soldier Review, 127 74th Street, North Bergen, New Jersey 07047, USA

Front cover, below Britains special production Royal Horse Guards. These delicately painted figures were cast and painted by Britains to the order of Mr Poitier-Smith. His collection was sold at Phillips in the 1970s and many of the items from it have re-appeared at auction. These five figures sold for £320/$576 in May 1988.

Back cover Britains were invited in 1924 to provide a box of toy soldiers for Queen Mary's dolls house. The result was this miniature display set, one sixth of standard size. The set presented to Queen Mary can be seen with her dolls' house at Windsor Castle. The set shown, the only other known, was given to the daughter of Frederick Britain, one of the Britains family. Her son sold this box at Phillips in June 1988 and the price was £3,500/$6,300.

Front cover, top A British Royal Horse Artillery team of the mid-nineteenth century made in wood and *papier maché* by Sonnenberg of Germany, 70 mm high. The horses are mounted on springs so that they appear to gallop. The painting is exquisitely doll-like, and the size foreshadows the multitude of Hausser and Lineol toys. Beautiful toy soldiers like these dating back to about 1870 are exceedingly rare, and these sold for £3,600/$6,480 at Phillips in January 1987.